Diggety Dog

Written by Michaela Morgan

Illustrated by Woody Fox

Diggety Dog dug a hole in the ground.
Dig,
　　　dig,
　　　　　dig,
　　　　　　　dig,
　　　　　　　　　dig.

I want to get
a bone that's big.

But this is what he found:

He found a big ugly bug,
who was stuck in a jug,
some spotty pants
and a greedy slug.

He found a very old clock,
tick tock, tick tock,
and a slithery snake
with a smelly sock.

Poo!

He met a happy rat,
a hen that said, "cluck,"
a lot of dizzy chicks
and a very cross duck.

There was a mole and a vole,
deep in the hole,
and a buzzy bee
with a cup of tea.

There was a crocodile,
who went snap, snap, SNAP!
And a sleepy mouse,
who wanted a nap.

He found a fox in green socks
and a frog with a flag,
a goat in a coat
and a crabby crab.

There was a toad in the hole
that said croak, croak, CROAK!
and a batty bat,
who liked a joke.

9

There was a blue kangaroo
that said, "Yoo hoo!"
and a mouse in a house
all alone.

Diggety was not happy.
He began to moan,
but then at last ...
... he found a big, big bone.

He dug and dug and dug.
Oh no!
Lots of bones.

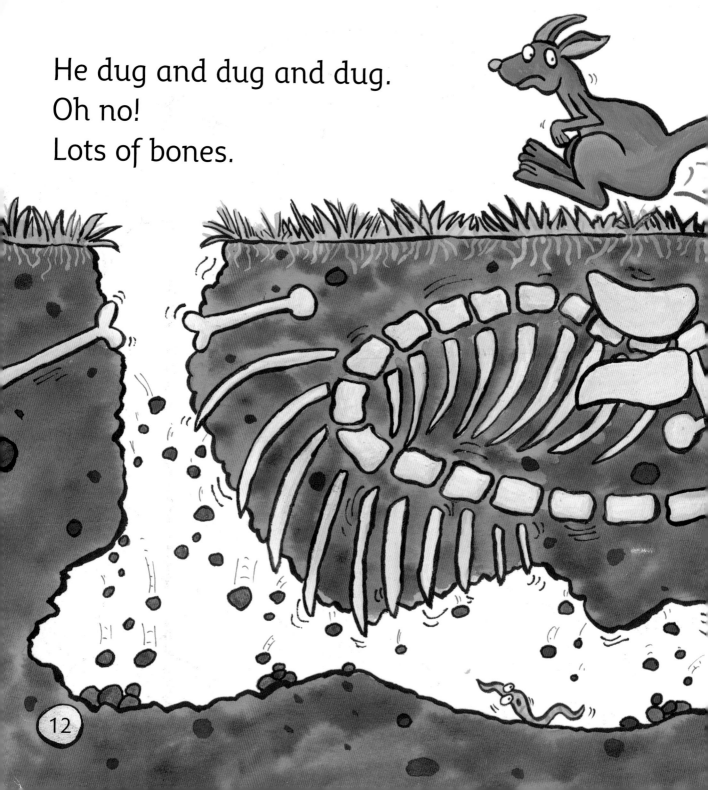

Diggety's hole

14

Ideas for reading

Learning objectives: Blend phonemes in words with clusters for reading; Hear, identify, segment and blend phonemes in words; Read high-frequency words and other familiar words on sight; Work out new words, and confirm or check meaning.

Curriculum links: Science: Plants and animals

Focus phonemes: y (ugly, spotty, greedy, very, smelly, slithery, happy, sleepy, dizzy), o-e (bone, mole, vole, joke)

Other new phonemes: ea, ie

Fast words: the, I, want, to, what, was, who, some, said, there, like(d), all, no, go

Word count: 215

Getting started

- Fast-read the words featuring the focus phonemes *y* and *o-e* using a small whiteboard. If children are experiencing any difficulties, show them how to blend through the words, sounding out the phonemes in the order in which they occur.

- Now write the irregular fast words, e.g. *want, some, said* and ask the children to fast-read them.

- Look at the front cover together. Invite them to read the title together. Demonstrate how to sound out the word 'Diggety'. Do the children think this is a real or made-up word? What do they think it means?

- This book is a rhyming text. See if children can help you make up other rhymes about Diggety Dog e.g. *Diggety Dog, lost in the fog.*

Reading and responding

- Give each child a copy of the book. Ask them to read it independently.

- Move around the group listening in on each child as they read. Can the children explain what *greedy slug, slithery snake* and *dizzy chicks* mean? Discuss any words that they are finding difficult to understand.

- Ask children who finish reading early to find their favourite page and read it aloud to their neighbour. They can explain why they like it too.